The Swing

JOE CEPEDA

ARTHUR A. LEVINE BOOKS

An Imprint of Scholastic Inc.

For the Avilas, the Olmedoses, the Gonzalezes, the Vonks, the Vasquezes, and for Cesar and Adriene.

Library of Congress Cataloging-in-Publication Data

Cepeda, Joe.

The swing / by Joe Cepeda. — 1st ed.   p. cm.

Summary: When Josey uses the new swing attached to the tree in her messy yard, she retrieves all the things her parents thought

they had lost over the years, including Leopoldo, their dog. ISBN 0-439-14260-1

[1. Lost and found possessions — Fiction. 2. Swings — Fiction. 3. Cleanliness — Fiction. 4. Neighbors — Fiction.] I. Title.

PZ7.C3184Swi 2006 [E] — dc22   2005024045   10 9 8 7 6 5 4 3 2 1   06 07 08 09 10

The display type is set in Hopper Josephine. The text type is set in Berliner Grotesk. Book design by Richard Amari

First edition, September 2006   Printed in Singapore 46

It was so embarrassing . . . another humiliation.
Josey's mom and dad sent Josey to borrow something
else. Again.
Josey's family never cleaned up the yard.

Her parents didn't throw nice parties, with invitations and everything.

People took down *their* holiday lights in January.

All the homes on her block looked freshly painted with bright, pretty, pastel colors like mint or aquamarine. Not Josey's.

Even worse, they lost things.

They lost Mr. Sandoval's popcorn popper.

They lost the camping gear they borrowed from the Guerreros. They lost Ms. Mangalang's favorite mixing bowl. And borrowed another.

They even lost their dog, Leopoldo.

What Josey hated most, though, was that her parents often lost track of time. Like today, Josey's dad promised to push her on the new swing, the one he strung up from the huge oak tree in the backyard, but he was too busy in the garage with Mr. Avila's lawn mower.

So Josey decided she could swing just fine on her own.

Slowly, she started to sway. Slowly, she pushed back her feet . . . then stretched them out and rocked back her body.

Faster with every thrust, she aimed for the highest branches.

With every push, Josey tried to lose herself among the lofty limbs.

Suddenly, she knocked something. "CLANK!"
A rusty piece of metal hit the ground.
Josey ran into the garage to show her dad.
"Where did you find this lantern?" he asked.
"Up there!" Josey pointed to the oak.

"Come on, Dad. Gimme a push!" A
few big shoves and she was back in
flight. Then, with one especially brave
and ultra-strong heave, Josey shot up
into the tree... and was gone!

Soon every branch and leaf trembled
and rattled like an enormous broken
washing machine.

Then the oak tree spit Josey out like
a lost sock.

"Are you all right?" her dad asked.
Josey straightened up, reached into the
crook of her arms, and pulled out . . .

"Our old toaster!" yelled her dad.

Josey hopped back on her swing.

"There's more, Dad!"

Her dad pushed. Josey swung. Off into the leafy green atmosphere Josey went.

Soon the whole neighborhood rumbled, and houses shook in their frames.
Down came Josey. With each trip they found more. Mom's wedding dress,
Josey's pogo stick, the family photo album . . .

Ernesto, the boy next door, was the first neighbor to join them. He sat next to Josey's dad and held on to him during the earthquakes every time Josey touched ground.

Ms. Mangalang found her favorite mixing bowl.
"Oh well, better late than never!" Everybody
laughed. "How about a Bundt cake?"
That's how the party started. When Josey

found guitar strings, her mom strummed some mean *rock en español.* Everyone covered their drinks each time the oak *piñata* shook, spilling out Josey and her loot.

And then, all of a sudden, the party stopped.
Josey stood by her swing . . . silent.

She turned to everyone and said, "There's one last thing. . . ." She looked
at her dad, and then to her neighbors. "I need your help."

They all followed her to the garage where she explained
what she needed.

But then Mr. Avila arrived. "Get away from
my lawn mower!" he shouted. Parts
were everywhere. "Please," said Josey.
"We're finding something." They all waited.
Finally, Mr. Avila looked at them and said,
"Someone hand me a hammer!" So they
all laughed and got back to work.
    After a while Josey yelled out to everyone,
"We're done!"

They rolled out the new contraption, a super-duper, gas-powered, *treasure-catching* swing! Everyone counted down.

"TEN!"

"NINE!"

"EIGHT!"

"SEVEN!"

"SIX!"

"FIVE!"

"FOUR!" Josey's dad revved the engine.

"THREE!"

"TWO!"

"ONE!"

In a blare of mechanical thunder, Josey vanished into the dense mysterious green.

While everyone watched, the grand old oak shook and rattled every limb. Frightened leaves rained down all over the yard. They could hear the swing roaring back and forth. The giant tree bent from side to side.

Then, the tree spit Josey out one last time. Down she crashed with . . .

. . . Leopoldo!

Neighbors scrambled out of the way as he bounded toward the food. Leopoldo wasn't done until he had licked every familiar face.

At dusk, Josey and her mom and dad watched as their friends walked down the block to their own homes with their own backyard trees.

Later they all took Leopoldo for a walk down the block.

"Need something?" asked Mr. Avila.

"We've got everything we need, thank you," said Josey.

"Woof!" said Leopoldo.